FREEDOM TO SERVE

What, who, and *how* you need to run
your ministry's finances so you
can focus on your calling

Jonathan Ankney

ISBN 13: 978-0999643006
ISBN 10: 0999643002

Tower Ministry Finance
44-03 48th Avenue, #130
Woodside, NY 11377

www.TowerMinistryFinance.com

With love and thanks to my
Big Sister and Big Brother-in-Law, Kim and Bruce.

Table of Contents

CONTEXT

In the spring of 1954 the Viet Minh—the League for the Independence of Vietnam—was finally poised to wrestle control of Vietnam from French control, a goal set during the group's formation in the mid-1930s. Standing in the way was General Henri Navarre, artillery commander Lieutenant Colonel Charles Piroth, and the battle-hardened French troops stationed at Dien Bien Phu. General Navarre's goal was to cut off the supply lines to the Viet Minh and force them into battle where victory would be won with superior fire power.

General Navarre's strategy backfired on him spectacularly. Piroth's initial artillery barrage failed to rout the Viet Minh in the early days of the battle, and after apologizing to his fellow officers for the unsuccessful effort, he returned to his bunker, held a grenade to his chest, pulled the pin, and committed suicide. The numerically superior Viet Minh, led by General Vo Nguyen Giap, literally dug into the surrounding mountains, and destroyed both airfields at the outpost and cargo planes on the tarmac at the onset.

The siege continued over the next two months as the Viet Minh tightened the noose on all sides. Vietnamese anti-aircraft guns picked off cargo planes that attempted landing, forcing the French to attempt parachuting supplies for their troops instead. This too backfired; the Viet Minh captured an estimated half of the food and ammunition dropped—literally starving French troops while beefing up their own stockpiles.

After nearly two months of steady depletion, the French succumbed and Dien Bien Phu fell. The French lost an estimate of 2,000 dead, 6,000 wounded, 1,700 missing, and 11,000 captured. The French withdrew from Vietnam in August, the country was divided in two at the Geneva Conference, and the stage was set for political upheaval that would ultimately lead the United States into war in 1959.

❖ ❖ ❖

One must wonder what it is like for a soldier to be under siege. The enemy inching closer and closer. Ammunition limited as food dwindles. Sleep, already difficult without the convenience of a bed, likely becoming more and more fitful as the stress increases. Meanwhile, non-combatant soldiers far behind the front are strategizing on how to get precious supplies through enemy lines to resupply the infantry. Back at the garrison, increasingly desperate soldiers turn their attention from battle to foraging for food and ammunition.

It's with this mindset of battle, front-line soldiers, supporting crew, and supplies that provide the context of this book. Administrative staff, church suppliers, lay leaders, church boards, trustees, and committee members are not on the front line or might only occasionally visit the front line. But just as a soldier at the front needs behind-the-lines support, ministers, youth pastors, counselors, social workers, and a host of others are more effective in spiritual battle when they focus their attention on service instead of logistics.

Perhaps you are on the front line—a minister or leading a ministry, and as soldier / leader you are trying to understand how to create a structure that supports you and your front-line team so that your ministry has the greatest impact possible. Perhaps you are, like me, in the business of supporting those at the front. Either way, we are in the same army, serving the same Master, and each must use our "different gifts, according to the grace given to each of us" to forward the mission of the Church.

If you are on the front line, you need to have the peace of mind knowing that there's money in the bank, that you can get supplies you and your team need, and that your donors can give with the confidence they'll receive acknowledgement and a tax receipt at the end of the year. Without this confidence, we end up with "head trash" that distract us from filling our core role, and we burn time that should have been used for ministry or to give ourselves much needed respite from the demands on our bodies and souls.

The goal of this book is to equip you with information about how to manage finances without getting technical. Let's leave the technical aspects to the technicians and focus on what you and the organization need to conduct business with the people and budget available for financial management. Every organization is going to be different in what it does and how it does things. However, there are basic components to what every organization needs in order to complete its work, and this book can be viewed as an enhanced checklist of what it takes to get the job done.

The structure of the book is straightforward. We first look at *what* we need to manage our finances. We need to conduct ministry affairs even if we're launching or rebuilding our financial team, so we need accounts and systems right away. Then we look at *who* we need to help the ministry so that a supporting team is ready. Then we look at *how* we bring everything together and *how* we should manage our finances.

In each case, I write the rationale behind my recommendation. Understanding why we do what we do helps us do it better. For example, over the decades I never gave any thought as to why highly liturgical churches read the Gospel lesson in the middle of the congregation. Then I joined a church that not only did that, but explained why it did so: the Word became flesh and dwelt among us. Now every Sunday, as the entire congregation focuses their attention on a priest, cross, and candles in the middle of an old nave, my appreciation for what has unfolded in front of me has deepened. Likewise, I want for your understanding about what is necessary to give you the freedom to conduct ministry to be clear and deep as possible.

Since this book is ultimately about taking action, we end by giving you a guideline on how to *execute* what you've learned and the *resources* that will help you and your team carry out the work you have been given to do.

WHAT

The first thing to look at is *what* we need to conduct our ministry. We start here for two reasons. The first reason is because it sometimes takes us a long time to find *who* we need to do the work. While we are looking for who will help us, we can make a lot of progress on what we need. Further, we need to have structure in place before we can make final decisions about how we are going to use those. So we start with what.

And what do we need? In principle we need to execute transactions and record those transactions. Executing means making sure that money changes hands and that goods and services are offered or received. When we place an order with the American Bible Society, we are making a transaction. When a donor sends us money, we are also making a transaction. That is execution.

But it is not enough to just execute transactions; we also need to record those transactions. Recording will give us a history of our activities that we will summarize in our financial reports, which allow us to analyze giving and spending trends, and gives us historical data that we can look up when there are questions about how we have conducted business.

The level of sophistication required varies by the size of the ministry, the number of transactions we have, and the type of ministry we operate. For example, a multi-campus church with millions of dollars in revenues will have a very different financial infrastructure than a community thrift store. In my for-profit work, I see differences between the solo law practitioner with a bank account and accounting software;

the ice cream shop with registers, gift card tracking, and their bank account; and the online business that only receives online payments and automates all of the payments it makes.

These systems typically become more helpful and run without much attention as they become more complex, but that leads to a new challenge: they must be properly configured during installation so that they work correctly and accept, distribute, and report funds in the manner they are intended to. Otherwise, they do an efficient job of making a terrible mess of things, just like my power saw does when I fail to set the correct cut width and depth. This means that, while you may be getting your tools in place now absent a full team, you'll either need to fully understand how these tools function, or you'll want someone on your team who can support you as you assemble them.

A typical ministry will have the following components that, to the extent it is feasible, are connected so that execution and recording are as automated as possible:

- Bank account
- Merchant systems to collect money
- Donor tracking systems
- Payment systems for expenses
- Payroll system
- General ledger system (accounting software)
- Budgeting system

Let's take a look at each.

Bank Account

The bank account truly is the ministry's storehouse. This is where we deposit funds, and from which we pay our expenses. At the risk of sounding too indifferent about bank accounts, the reality is that these days there is not much difference between banks. Later on, I speak about the importance of a good banker, but for now I will point out that the qualities of a good bank account are based around ease-of-use and whatever interest can be gained. If you are unhappy with your bank and there is a better option available to you, then perhaps it's time to consider changing banks. It's not hard to change, but it does needs to be done with some forethought.

Questions to ask about your bank account:
- Do I find it easy to make deposits and to issue payments?
- Is the bank interested in the well-being of our ministry?
- To what extent is the for-profit business interested in a religious organization, and is the bank able and willing to support our work?

Electronic Payment Systems

Electronic payment systems (merchant services) allow businesses and ministries to collect money electronically, outside of the bank account. The two most common that we think of are credit card / debit card giving and automated clearing house (ACH) giving. There are many services and many options available. Some options have an integrated interface with the service, and other options allow for a different interface to integrate with the payment system, such as the donor tracking system, which we will discuss next. For purposes of this discussion, we are not concerned with the technical side of things. What we are concerned about is the ability to receive money electronically.

As we think about electronic payment systems, we should be mindful of the following features:

The ability to *accept different payment types*. Not only do we want to be able to generally receive credit card, debit card, and ACH payments, but we should consider which cards we can accept, for example.

We also want to consider *ease of use* from the donor's perspective. After all, they are already giving us their money, so it would be best that we not ask them to give more of their time simply to make a payment!

Every merchant service charges *fees* for their role in collecting and processing money, so we want to consider how much those fees are. The service needs to be very transparent about what those fees will be, and then give monthly statements so we can confirm what those fees actually were. Fees are typically going to run 3%± depending on the service. Some platplatforms charge more due to additional services they offer. This is especially the case for services that assist with fundraising campaigns.

It is especially helpful to have giving systems integrate with *donor systems*. This saves the ministry time and money from additional personnel expense to record contributions in the donor system.

A great merchant service will provide statements or other tools that make it *easy to reconcile* income and understand how much they are holding for processing. A merchant service is effectively an intermediary bank. A donor may give money on a Sunday, but the ministry may not see it until Tuesday or Wednesday. Where is that money? Well, it is in the merchant's bank. The merchant received it immediately, but since it is still in process and not reaching the ministry's bank until later in the week, it remains in that merchant's bank. Since the merchant is holding that money, and since it is effectively an intermediary bank, wouldn't it be helpful to know how much it is holding? That is the reason for having reconciliation tools.

Another factor to consider is the *speed* with which the merchant will get the money from the donor to you. As you talk to merchant services, be sure to ask how long it takes for them to process and get the money into your bank.

And finally, make sure that the service offers good *support*. This will save the ministry time when the inevitable problem happens, and it will help the ministry's reputation with donors when you can get back to them quickly after they have an issue or problem with giving.

Questions to ask about incoming payment systems:
- Does the payment system make it easy for donors to give?
- Does the payment system give us reports that help us confirm the accuracy of income as reported on our general ledger's financial report?
- How quickly does the money reach our bank once the donor gives?
- How are fees compared to other payment systems?

Donor Tracking

Now that we have thought about where to store the money and how to receive the money, let's think a little bit about how to record these transactions—our donor tracking system. Donor tracking has a number of different useful functions.

From an accounting standpoint, being able to identify the source of the income, when it was received, what it was intended for, and then compare donor tracking to our financial reports are all useful functions. From a financial planning and fundraising standpoint, it helps to identify who the major donors are and where they are investing in ministry, as well as identify individuals and organizations that have given in the past and may be primed to increase their gifts. From a tax compliance standpoint, donor systems allow us to prepare receipts and annual statements that allow us to confirm receipt of funds so that donors can report charitable contributions to the IRS and use them to reduce their taxable income.

At minimum, a donor tracking system will record the donor name, donation date, amount, and designations. This information is enough for us to prepare the statements and give us the basics about who is giving, why they are giving, and how to review timing trends. Knowing designation is especially helpful for those instances when we need to deal with donor stipulations. For example, donors may designate contributions for specific ministries, missionaries, or programs within a church or ministry. Such stipulations may require the organization to confirm that the money that was received was used as the donor requested. There are specific IRS rules and guidelines that must be followed in such instances, and the donor tracking system should be capable of tracking these types of designations.

A donor tracking system should also have features that allow the ministry to easily account for income. Donor systems should have areas to specify the type of income as reported on financial reports, the payment method, and where the money was deposited. This allows the financial team to confirm that the amounts reported on financial reports are the same as those received through the donor system. In fact, in some cases the accounting system does not record individual donations. Instead, the bookkeeper will look at the total from the donor tracking system and enter that into the accounting system to record the revenue. This way, the donor system becomes a subsidiary part of the accounting system.

With the advent of digital imaging, donor systems can now also keep pictures of checks and donor correspondence instead of needing paper files. This saves bookkeeping staff the time of physically storing and retrieving documents. Additionally, it saves on storage space—an issue for ministries that do not have much room in their facilities.

Often a donor system will have the built-in tools to integrate with electronic payment services. This is especially convenient for both the donor and the staff: the donor logs onto a website or uses an app on their phone to initiate the transaction, while the staff doesn't need to get involved in the processing. It's all recorded digitally. If the owner system is integrated with the accounting software, then record-keeping is also much easier. Even if it is not fully integrated, a donor system that allows access to data might allow users to regularly export data and import it into the accounting system, thereby speeding up entry through importing as opposed to typing. For example, I worked with a programmer to create a daily import file for one of my clients. The program he developed would access the donor data every night and create a summary of it that the accounting software could import. We estimate that this saved 1½ to two hours daily—effectively giving the staff an additional day per week to take on more work.

Finally, donor tracking software should be able to report in summary format and detailed format any of the information that it keeps in the database. I find it especially helpful to be able to export data out of the database into a spreadsheet and then do analysis to compare what is in the donor system to the data in the accounting software.

Questions to ask about incoming payment systems:
- Does the payment system make it easy for donors to give?
- Does the payment system give us reports that help us confirm the accuracy of income as reported on our general ledger's financial report?
- How quickly does the money reach our bank once the donor gives?
- How are fees compared to other payment systems?

Expense Payment Systems

Now that we've covered what we need to collect money, let's think about what we need to pay expenses. In general we want to be able to pay for things quickly and easily, retain receipts or other proofs that the expenses were paid, and to convey to the accounting team the information they need to record the transaction.

There are a number of ways to achieve these tasks:
- paying by cash
- paying with checks
- paying with credit cards
- paying by debit cards
- paying with prepaid debit cards
- paying via wires
- paying online via the bank's bill pay system
- using a bill payment service

While payroll is a form of expense payment, I am addressing it in the next section since it exists in a special world of its own.

<u>Payment by Cash</u>
Paying expenses by cash is the second oldest method in the book—right after paying for things with pelts and sea shells. As such, it is common for ministries to keep a little bit of cash on hand to pay for small expenses, such as emergency office supplies and other things where cash makes sense.

While paying with cash is very convenient, it does come with its own hazards. First, it is not uncommon to find that there is a discrepancy between how much cash should be on hand and how much cash actually is on hand. In unfortunate incidents, this occurs because someone has been stealing the money. What I see more frequently is simply a lack of paying attention to details and giving receipts for expenses. Without the receipts, we don't know what the money was actually used for, and it always raises the question as to whether or not it is mere forgetfulness or if someone really is taking the money.

Payments by Checks

Paying for expenses by check is probably the least convenient for staff, but it allows for the accounting team to track expenses best. This is true because accounting has far more control over how the money is spent and how it is reported before it issues the check. Nearly every other payment method allows for the spending to be done first, and then accounting chases down staff to ask questions about details that staff may not feel are important anymore. In contrast, when staff are in a hurry to get a check from accounting, they're much more willing to comply with requests for clarifying information from the accounting team.

Checks can either be printed or handwritten. In the case of printing, the check information is first entered into the accounting software. After the staff has entered information for all the checks that need to be printed, blank check stock is put into the printer and the printing process is completed. This is most common in organizations where the number of checks issued is high and / or frequent. For organizations where checks are handwritten, the check is written and then the information is manually entered into the accounting software.

Payments by Credit Card

If you and your staff are doing a lot of running around outside of the office, it is very helpful to have credit cards. These are quite convenient to have because it allows the staff the freedom to make purchases without having to wait for checks or cash to be handed to them. The downside is that the organization loses some control over spending. This can be mitigated by specifying the types of expenses that are authorized to the staff and the amount of money that they can spend.

A convenient tool that helps monitor credit card spending and adds control is Expensify. This service allows cardholders to log into a website, categorize their spending, and submit their expenses for supervisor review. After the supervisor has reviewed and approved the spending, the accounting staff digitally imports the transaction data into the accounting software. As one might imagine, this adds multiple layers of convenience, including having the cardholder categorize their expenses, having the supervisor review and authorize expenses, and reducing data entry for the accounting staff.

Payments by Debit Card

Debit cards act just like credit cards with one significant difference for financial management: whereas credit cards allow ministries to build up a tab and then pay it all at once, debit cards pull money from the bank immediately. If the ministry cannot get credit cards, then this would be an alternative to consider.

Payments by Prepaid Debit Card

Another alternative to credit cards to consider are prepaid debit cards. A prepaid card is issued to each cardholder, and the organization can transfer money from the bank to each cardholder's prepaid account. Limits can be made on what staff can purchase, and because it is a prepaid card, the spending limit has effectively been predetermined.

Payments by Wire or ACH

If the ministry is trying to move money quickly or has a large amount to pay and does not want to issue a check, then a wire or ACH transaction is the most likely way to go. There are two downsides to these methods that I have seen. The first is that the sender and the receiver typically both pay substantial fees for the convenience, especially for the wire. The second downside is that these are issued from the bank, typically requiring signatories' time to authorize the transfers.

Payments by Bank Bill Pay

As online banking becomes more common, we are seeing more and more payments being made directly from banks. When this is done, the bank sends a check on behalf of the ministry, and the money is drawn from the bank on the date of the check. While it does not happen often, I have seen instances where the recipient has not received the money even though the bill payment was issued and the money drawn from the originating account. When this happens, it can become very frustrating because in the originator's mind the bill has been paid, when in reality the obligation has not been fulfilled since the recipient has not received the funds.

Payments by Bill Payment Service
Bill payment services act a lot like bank bill pays, only on steroids. These services will mail out checks on behalf of organizations, and unlike bank bill payment systems, they allow for additional features, including multiple levels of authorization and adding accounting information that can be electronically exported to the organization's accounting software. This would allow remote staff to prepare payments, then get supervisory approval for issuing the payment, and then save the bookkeeper time from having to enter accounting information and physically preparing the check.

Questions to ask about outbound payment systems:

- Do the payment systems make it easy, within the boundaries of authorization and control, for staff to make payments?
- Are we able to implement controls to ensure that staff members are spending appropriately for the ministry and within limits that the board and executive team have established?
- Is the financial team able to monitor spending and know the details of the purchases—who, when, how much, and for what purpose?

Payroll

Payroll is very complex and specialized, so it merits discussion outside of all other expenses. It is complex for two basic and related reasons. The primary reason is that employers become collections agents for the State courtesy of withholding taxes. When a payroll is run, a significant percentage of an employee's compensation never gets to them because the government requires employers to withhold a portion of each employee's compensation and turn it over as an installment on the annual tax bill. The State tends to view employers as being sophisticated and in complete control of finances, so governments expect employers to be able to accurately calculate the taxes and pay them on time. This is the first reason.

The second reason is the complexity of the taxes themselves. Each state has different tax laws that can change without warning and tend to be complex. In some cases, taxes are interrelated. Just last week, I saw an example of how these different complexities can sometimes occur. A client was asking me why certain paychecks were lower than they had been the previous month. Well, the City of New York decided to change rates in the middle of the year. As a result, more taxes were withheld, lowering the net pay. Another client received a notice saying that they underpaid a certain type of tax, and that was because they could not claim credit because they underpaid another tax.

Employers have a number of different options to choose from when it comes to payroll. Let's take a look at each option, starting from the most "do-it-yourself" form to the most "I don't want to think about it" service.

Manual Calculations

In the manual calculation scenario, the ministry would not rely on any service and would do all of the calculations itself. The government provides documents that explain how payroll tax is calculated, and the ministry is responsible for referencing those documents, calculating the taxes, initiating the tax payments, and filing payroll tax returns with each applicable government agency. With so many other options, some of which are quite inexpensive, there is really no reason to go this route. In my decades of work, I have never come across a ministry or business that annually calculates payroll. I have, however, used payroll tax manuals in order to occasionally help ministry leaders and their staff at the beginning of the year when they are trying to figure out how much their withholdings should be.

Payroll Calculator Software

The next option we have is to purchase software or subscribe to an online service that calculates the payroll taxes on our behalf. These services track tax calculations and laws for you so that you don't have to. When it comes time to run payroll, the ministry enters in the compensation amount for each person, and the software calculates all the taxes. The ministry is responsible for making timely tax payments and for filing tax returns and other documents.

This effectively covers the second layer of complexity mentioned earlier: the complexity of the calculations. Payroll services handle all of the work of reading the tax laws and tax manuals so that you don't have to. What you still have to do is worry about the first level of tax complexity, which is being a good agent for the State.

These services are rather inexpensive and are a good option if the ministry has a person who is able to keep on top of the filings and "agent" type of activities with the knowledge and expertise required to deal with problems that inevitably arise on the agency side of payroll transactions.

This option comes in both personal computer and online versions, and it is available as standalone software or integrated into the accounting software. The personal computer / standalone system would mean that the ministry installs the software onto the computer, and then after each payroll, the bookkeeper needs to type the information into the accounting software. The personal computer / integrated setup means that the ministry would purchase the payroll software as an additional module to the accounting software they currently use. The advantage to the integrated setup is that there is no need to retype any information. Once payroll is run, it already shows up in the financial reports.

Similarly to the desktop version, the online version has both standalone and integrated options. The online / standalone service has the user login, enter the information, and annually put payroll information into the accounting software, which could be another online service or a desktop accounting application. The online / integrated service would be similar in that the bookkeeper would login online to enter payroll information—hours, reimbursements, etc.—and that information would be exported to the accounting software.

In this case, the accounting software could be either online or desktop versions.

Payroll Calculator Plus Filings
The next level of service would be described as "payroll calculator on steroids." More specifically, the payroll service not only offers the calculator, but it also offers to assist or execute the filings for the ministry. This covers a significant portion of the services that most ministries need. However, it does not include support when the IRS or state tax agencies contact the ministry with questions, issues, or proposed penalties. In theory, these notices would be few and far between at this level of service because the payroll service will be making the filings for the ministry. Nevertheless, these still come up from time to time, and it would be the ministry's responsibility to deal with them.

Payroll Calculator, Filings, Tax Support
This service is almost everything the ministry requires. The ministry only needs to provide the service with the hours for hourly staff and any salary changes. With this information, the payroll service calculates the payroll, makes the tax filings automatically, and its tax department responds to any tax notices that the ministry receives. Upon setting up the ministry as a new client, payroll services typically set up the tax documentation so that they automatically receive notices from the IRS and state tax agency. Thus, they are tuned into whatever is happening with taxes on behalf of the ministry.

Depending on the service, there are different options for integrating with the accounting software. Some of the largest services are not associated with any type of accounting software, but they do offer data export services that allow ministries to export each payroll in a data file and import it into their accounting system.

Professional Employer Organization

The last payroll option is one that is rather interesting. There are businesses known as professional employer organizations (PEOs) that exist for the sole purpose of being the employer of record in the IRS's eyes. The way it works is that a ministry has employees that report to managers and the executive director, pastor, or executive pastor all for the purpose of functioning in the ministry. But from an *employment* standpoint, the PEO becomes the surrogate employer. Functionally the ministry is operating with its entire staff, yet financially, all staff members are part of another corporation that exists solely for the purpose of compensating them.

The upside to this type of service is that everything related to payroll, compensation, and benefits is handled by the professional employer organization. Often, the service can use its large pool of "staff" (including multiple ministries and businesses) to get the best rates on various insurances and other benefits. The downside to the professional employer organization is that they can be expensive. Nevertheless, they are an option and are popular enough to merit mentioning.

So these are your basic payroll options. The ministry is going to have a price to pay, either in time or in money. I offer these options so that you can be thinking about the best balance for your ministry. Most of my clients use a full-service payroll service. It is also the option that I use for my business. Tax notices are few and far between, but when they come, they can be very distracting, stressful, and time-consuming to address. As such, most people prefer receiving the maximum level of service from their payroll service so that they can continue to stay focused on what matters most: the ministry.

Finally, it is *imperative* that payroll be set up correctly from the start. Errors in payroll configuration can prove costly in two ways. First, correcting errors can be complicated and take a lot of time to correct. Each payroll needs to be reviewed to see who was affected, what parameter was incorrect, the amount that needs to be corrected, and from there, the payroll service must be contacted in order to understand the steps to correction. Most likely, amended tax returns must be prepared, and filed with the appropriate tax agencies. Second, there will be fees associated with the correction if payroll taxes are affected. At minimum there will be amended return preparation fees to the payroll service, and possibly interest and penalties to government agencies. Correct payroll configuration is one of the essentials when starting payroll or changing payroll services and should not be done without expert guidance.

Questions to ask about payroll:

- How easy is it for the bookkeeper to prepare a payroll?
- How easy is it for the bookkeeper to get payroll numbers into the accounting software?
- Do the reports tell us enough information about our payroll costs and tax liabilities so that we understand how we're operating against budget and whether or not we have a significant run-up of tax obligations?
- How much do we feel we can take on payroll responsibilities?

Visit www.TowerMinistryFinance.com/FreedomToServe to see how payroll and payroll taxes work.

Budgeting System

The budgeting system is typically included in the accounting software. Its purpose is to create a forecast financial statement to show what we expect to receive in terms of income and how much we plan on spending. This forecast is very important for ministry because it shows the financial implications of our fundraising efforts and how we plan on using that money to perform ministry. Making ministry plans without a budget means that we are making decisions inside of a vacuum without considering how it might impact us financially. As we all know, ignorance is not bliss, and not estimating the financial impact could end up hurting a ministry should it run out of money.

In practice, different parts of the budget are typically created in spreadsheets by pastors, ministry leaders, and other people of responsibility. Once this is done, the individual budgets are reviewed by the financial head, finalized, and compiled into a master budget. This is the budget that goes into the budget system.

Once the budget is in the budget system, the finance head can easily produce reports to see how well a ministry is doing against its forecast. If there is significant variance to the positive, then the ministry can think about what to do with the anticipated surplus. Perhaps it can add to reserves or it can initiate new ministries that have been on hold due to constraints. If the variance is significantly less, then the ministry will need to make choices about where to constrain spending in the immediate future while beefing up its fundraising efforts.

Questions to ask about budgeting system:
- How hard it is to set up a budget that works with our general ledger system?
- Can we import our templates into the budget system?
- Can we run different types of budget reports to see how our actual numbers are compared to what we had budgeted?

Visit www.TowerMinistryFinance.com/FreedomToServe to see examples of how budgets are created and used for managing ministries.

Accounting Software

The general ledger software, commonly described as the accounting software, is the backbone of the record-keeping system. Its core purpose is to collect and consolidate transaction data in order to produce reports for management and board so they can make strategic decisions. All of the transactions from the financial components need to be recorded in this software in some fashion. Perhaps all of the details of one type of system are entered here, such as the payroll system, or perhaps only summary information is entered. I often see donations entered into software in summary form. Whatever form it is, transactions need to show up in the accounting software. Then, once all the transactions have been recorded, reports are issued to inform the board and leadership team as to the state of the ministry.

The general ledger software is typically able to perform duties beyond just recordkeeping and reporting. Bill payment functions, asset tracking, and check writing features are all functions that general ledger software offers. However, the primary function of this software is to record and to report. If it cannot do either of these, it is of little use.

From a high level, the information it needs to track are a) things that represents the financial "net worth" of the ministry, such as all of our bank balances, credit card balances, payroll taxes due, asset values, liability balances, etc.; and b) things that tell us how much we made (donations received, grants received, fundraisers, etc.) and how we spent the money (payroll, facilities, ministry supplies, etc.). With this information, we are able to prepare a balance sheet and a profit and loss statement (which CPAs refer to as *Statement of Financial Position* and *Statement of Activity*, respectively, though the report names matter much less than the information contained in them).

In order to get this information, we need to have certain information from our transactions. At minimum we need a) the *date* of a transaction, b) the *"who"* of the transaction (who gave us money or who we paid), c) *how much money* was in the transaction, and d) what the *accounting breakdown* was (the bank or credit card account, the income or expense account, and if the details of the transaction needs to be split out).

Some information can be summarized in the general ledger. For example, a ministry may decide that the general ledger only needs to summary information for its entire payroll in the general ledger and on the financial reports as opposed to individual paychecks. Alternatively, there are so many donors and donations that the donor system holds the details and only a summary entry is made into the general ledger. It is perfectly normal to have details in one system and a summary entry in the general ledger. In fact, I have found that it is better to have separate "best of breed" components instead of one piece of software that does everything at a mediocre level. If you decide to do this for your own church or ministry, then it will be important to check the detailed numbers and the summary general ledger information to make sure that they are accurate.

Since all accounting software needs to have the same core accounting features, I typically look for two non-accounting features to see if the software is qualified to work with. First, is it easy to use? Is the interface user-friendly? Is it easy to see where to enter or retrieve information? Is it easy on the eyes? These questions are going to help because we are looking at the ease of input. Then second, how easy is it to read the financial reports? Is the data formatted clearly? Can we understand how the ministry is doing in a short period of time, or will we have to hunt around to find information? Can we easily configure reports to our liking, by changing fonts and how we categorize information? Each accounting package is going to have a statement of financial position and statement of activity, but not all reports are created equal! Some will be easier to read than others. These are all related to the speed of retrieving information.

Finally, the question may arise as to which software to use. Most of the ministries I speak to use either QuickBooks Desktop or QuickBooks Online. The minor downside to these packages is that they are not specifically designed for nonprofit environments, which have some unique accounting and reporting needs. The major upside is that they are easy to use and are so prevalent that it is easy to find bookkeepers qualified to do the bookkeeping work. Further, there are ways to configure both packages so that we can track designated funds and do other tasks specific to the nonprofit environment.

Questions to ask about your accounting software:

- Is this software easy for the bookkeeper to use?
- If the bookkeeper leaves, how hard will it find some-one to replace them with someone that understands the software?
- In the event that the bookkeeper is temporarily gone, is it easy enough to understand that someone else can do basic tasks?
- Do the reports summarize information clearly enough that the executive team, finance committee, and board understand what is happening and can make key policy and strategic decisions?

NOTES

NOTES

_____

_____

_____

_____

_____

_____

_____

_____

_____

_____

_____

WHO

Now that we have talked about the "what" of financial ministry, we can now address the "who" of financial ministry. It is not enough just to know *what* we need—we also need people. It makes me think of the new building that is going up on my street: tools, machinery, and building supplies were all delivered, but progress wasn't made until the foreman and construction crew showed up and began to use them.

In this section, we are going to look at the individuals who will use financial tools to create a financial structure. They will make it easier to see the money, to pay for things, to understand what our financial reports are telling us about our ministry, to comply with the law, to stay safe, and to maximize employee compensation within our budget.

Depending on your church or ministry, some of these individuals may be full-time, some may be part-time, all might be part-time, and some people may even take on multiple financial roles. How much each person works doesn't matter, and how the work is divided or combined doesn't matter. What does matter is that your ministry has the team and coverage it needs to get the job done, and that you are able to have them for as long as you need. How much time they spend will be determined by how large and sophisticated the ministry is. Let's first think about who we need before worrying about the details.

Every church and ministry needs to have the following in order to meet its core financial function:
- Bookkeeper
- General accountant
- Chief financial officer
- Finance committee
- Liability insurance broker
- Lawyer

In addition, the ministry may want to have the following go-to people as part of its finance team:
- Banker
- Investment advisor
- Certified Public Accountant (CPA)
- Clergy / personal tax advisor
- HR consultant
- Benefits advisor(s) (health insurance, retirement, etc.)

Let's look at each to see how they contribute to financial ministry.

Bookkeeper

A good bookkeeper is invaluable to the organization that they serve. They are the primary financial eyes and ears of the ministry, seeing details that few ever see. Because they are so close to the details, they are also the first line of defense for spotting problems and anomalies.

By definition, a bookkeeper will "keep the books" by recording transactions and doing their role to make sure that the information is as accurate as possible. Typically though, a bookkeeper is going to handle more than that.

First, and even before transactions can be recorded, a bookkeeper helps make transactions. They prepare checks, give petty cash to other staff, contact the credit card company to issue and terminate cards, prepare wires, help donors when there are contribution issues, prepare payroll, and anything else that facilitates the movement of money.

Second, they do the record-keeping. This may mean typing, accessing another piece of software to initiate import into the general ledger, and reviewing their work to ensure accuracy and comparing the books to the bank to ensure that all transactions are ready for review by their manager.

Third, a bookkeeper typically does a lot of mundane financial administration—opening the mail, replying to inquiries from vendors about payment status, replacing lost vendor checks, filing, etc.

Because a bookkeeper is so important in an organization, it is important to know what qualities to look for when hiring them. I often describe good bookkeepers as good soldiers: they need to understand and follow the processes that financial managers have set up; they need to process paperwork fast. They should possess excellent typing skills in both speed and accuracy, and they need to have an eye for detail in order to notice problems. Additionally, they need to know how to respond to issues and have the discretion to know when they should respond on their own and when they should raise the matter to their superior.

When it comes to recruiting, the best advice comes from the title of a book written by entrepreneur and recruiting consultant Mel Kleiman: *Hire Tough, Manage Easy*. It's not enough to look at resumes, ask a few questions, and get glowing references from people that prospective bookkeepers are friends or colleagues with. We need to test them to see if their bookkeeping, typing, and organizational skills are as good as they claim. Some of the most painful mistakes I have made in my own business were from relying on resumes, interviews, and references to screen applicants. It wasn't until I began to test them with an assessment I created that I successfully filtered qualified people into my business. After initiating testing, I have gone on to successfully recruit solid performers for my clients. This is not to say that we can't trust applicants or we are assuming that they are liars. At the same time, we cannot assume that their self-assessment is the same standard as what we need. With testing, we can follow the words of Ronald Reagan: "trust, but verify."

I should make one final point about bookkeepers: it's not entirely necessary to have a professional bookkeeper assist your organization. I've had a number of instances with both ministry and for-profit clients where administrative staff did basic bookkeeping as part of their jobs. In fact, I would rather train an amateur with the right aptitude than work with a trained bookkeeper with poor and sloppy habits.

There are three factors that make this type of situation work. First, there needs to be consistent processes that they follow. This means that donor income is recorded the same way every time, that vendor bills are paid the same way using the same expense account every month, and other financial processes have been firmly established. Second, they have to be sticklers for detail, both in the numbers and for following processes. Third, they really do need to be good typists and move quickly. Speed and accuracy make a considerable difference in productivity, and this is especially true when it comes to having people doing bookkeeping as one part of their responsibilities.

Questions to ask about your bookkeeper:
- Does our bookkeeper have the skills necessary to do their job quickly and accurately? If not,
  - What skills need to be improved?
  - What training is required to improve those skills?
- Does our bookkeeper have the aptitude necessary to get the job done?
- Are we paying our bookkeeper too much or too little?

- If our bookkeeper suddenly went away, would we be able to figure out where things stood and resume operations quickly?

Visit www.TowerMinistryFinance.com/FreedomToServe for a sample bookkeeper job description.

Management Accountant

While a bookkeeper is invaluable as the eyes and ears of the financial ministry, we also need an overseer who can understand the big picture and guide the bookkeeper. This person would be responsible for setting up the accounting software, connecting the donor system, collections of systems, payment components, payroll, and budgeting with said software. They would also establish the processes that the ministry will use to execute transactions. Finally, they will guide the board and pastoral staff and policies that the ministry needs to set precedents for how the organization conducts business. It's God's business, but it's still business.

Who is this person? I'm going to introduce to you a new concept: the management accountant. When we normally think of accountants, we think of certified public accountants (CPA). Certified public accountants are accountants trained and tested on topics related to public accounting: how to audit publicly held companies, auditing public charities, and taxation. Their industry's rules require that they prepare financial reports in a rigid way so that every organization's financial reports appear the same way—so much so, that it is often difficult to understand exactly what the reports mean. To further exacerbate the problem, these rules are created by various committees and endorsed by a governing board of accountants.[1]

---

[1] I'm describing what is known as generally accepted accounting principles or GAAP. To give an idea as to how poorly this serves nonprofits, the Financial Accounting Standards Board (the accounting profession's policy-making body) requires that

As the legal profession has different specializations, the accounting profession also has specializations. There are accountants who are trained and certified in fraud, in treasury management, in government accounting, in forensic accounting, and so on. A management accountant specializes in accounting that is specific to management's needs. This means that they are trained in budgeting, cash flow forecasting, setting up internal financial controls, operations, and preparing financial reports for the leadership team.

With this in mind, we can see why a management accountant would be the logical choice for working with the bookkeeper. Most ministries would prefer the individual whose loyalty is to leadership and is thinking internal function over someone whose loyalty is to the general public and imposes onerous rules.

---

nonprofits' expenses be reported in a format that requires only *three* functional categories: program services, fundraising, and general management. That's it. There's no requirement to provide a report format that presents classifications such as payroll, utilities, travel, etc. In practice, certified public accountants will walk into an organization, take the statement of activities (profit and loss report) that is readable by leadership and the board, and reformat and reorganize that same information into a standard format that few people can read. The better ones will prepare an additional report to show a more detailed breakdown, but that is not required. As you can imagine, a financial report that only shows three expense lines would be of little use for managing and guiding a church or ministry.

This is not to say that a certified public accountant cannot do the role of a management accountant. There are people who are capable of fulfilling both roles, and many CPAs have transitioned their careers into management accounting. *However, I am cautioning against assuming that a certified public accountant can and will perform the work of a management accountant.* The implication is that management needs to look carefully at people who come their way and ask themselves if these accountants have the experience and mindset of a management accountant. If they do, that's great. If they do not have this experience and mindset, then there's a talent gap that needs to be bridged.

Questions to ask about your financial manager:
- Do we have someone who sees the big picture of our ministry's financial system?
- When one of our components breaks down, who steps in to fix it?
- Do we have someone with management experience to provide accounting and finance-specific direction to the bookkeeper?

Chief Financial Officer

A number of years ago a friend asked me what the difference was between accounting and finance. The answer I gave then holds true today, and it is applicable to us as we work through who we need to effectively manage our finances. The difference between accounting and finance is that accounting is focused on reporting about the past, while finance is about taking what we have and growing in the future.

This difference was very real to me in my early days of business school when I was considering whether or not to do a concentration in finance or accounting. My advisor recommended that I speak to both the accounting professor and the finance professor, which I did, and both of them recommended that I study accounting. Why? Because both the finance professor and the accounting professor held the position that nonprofit organizations needed people to track money, but people who could estimate the future benefit of spending were unnecessary. Yet contrary to their advice, and in a moment of mild rebellion that I don't understand to this day, I ignored them both and chose finance.

Upon graduation I met with the finance professor and explained what I learned about finance's application to the nonprofit world. What I learned was that nonprofit organizations *must* be thinking about impact—about what is known in the for-profit world as *return on investment*. Unlike businesses that measure return in dollars, nonprofits measure return by lives changed: the number of refugees from North Korea now living free lives; the number of children educated; how many villages now have wells and residents who can live richer, fuller lives beyond merely searching for water; the number of women rescued from sex trafficking; or how many souls have been saved from addiction and found peace with God. The list could go on and on.

So this bears the question: who in your church and ministry helps you determine the least expensive way to deliver the greatest impact?

The reality is that having one person for this role is too much for many ministries. The budget isn't there, and the need for a full-time person really isn't there either. However, we still need to be thinking about return on investment. The answer for this role, if it isn't plausible as a full-time position, typically comes from three places.

First, the senior-most person in management needs to be able to wear a CFO hat and have an investment mentality. It might mean that they need some financial training they may or may not want, but the reality is that they will be better leaders and take the ministry further if they have this knowledge.

Second, the management accountant can help take on this role. In my outsourced CFO business, I typically end up doing a blended role of both financial advisor and management accountant. The management accountant in your own ministry is already comfortable with numbers, so they're an excellent person to go to for conversations about how much it would cost for a new initiative and what the impact would be.

Finally, the finance committee should always be strategically thinking about costs and ministry results. A good finance committee will use its collective experience and brainpower to support these decisions.

One last point: there most certainly are finance-specific topics beyond strategy and return on investment. Churches occasionally need financing due to cash flow needs, building projects, and thinking about risk. We cover much of this in this book, but if there's one thing I want to really emphasize in this section, it's that every ministry must be thinking about stewardship in its truest form: *what results are we seeing with the resources the Master has given us?*

Questions to ask about the CFO role:
- Do we have a "return on investment" mindset?
- Do we have someone available who will help us understand costs and what ministry impact we're getting from what we spend?
- Should we conduct any training for our leaders and staff to get them thinking about return on investment?

Treasurer

The ministry's treasurer is the board officer whose fiduciary responsibility is to guard the finances—the treasury—of the ministry. The ministry's by-laws should explicitly state how this person is selected, what their qualifications are, their responsibilities, and the length of their term.

Often the treasurer's role and focus changes depending on the size of the ministry. Smaller ministries will likely require that the treasurer be involved in the day-to-day affairs of the ministry, possibly even to the point of handling the bookkeeping. Treasurers at larger organizations with professional financial staff will be able to focus on policy, strategy, and occasionally special projects, such as capital budgeting, preparing special reports, or doing analysis on the organization's financials. A treasurer will interface with the board, the minister or executive director, and typically find occasion to work with the bank, the investment manager, insurance professionals, the auditors, the financial staff, and other financial professionals that support the ministry through financial talents.

The role of treasurer calls for a significant amount of balance and discretion. To the extent that they aren't involved in daily operations, the treasurer still needs to be aware of what is going on—monitoring the ministry to ensure that it is on track and that no problems are developing. The treasurer also needs to be able to look at the ministry from multiple perspectives in order to balance the demands of a limited budget, including the board's perspective, paid leadership's perspective, constituents' perspectives, and even different divisions within the ministry. Finally, treasurers need to balance their decision-making process and know when to trust the Holy Spirit and when to trust old-fashioned math.

Questions to ask about the treasurer:
- Do we have someone who has the financial knowledge to monitor our finances?
- Does this person think with their head and listen with their heart as they make recommendations and decisions about the ministry?
- Are they balanced in their approach and thinking to the challenges the ministry faces?
- Are they free of conflicts of interest?
- Are they articulate and able to communicate the ministry's needs and decisions?

Finance Committee

In the world of nonprofits, boards are legally charged with the fiduciary responsibility of stewarding the organization on behalf of its owners—the public. The finance committee is the group of individuals whose responsibility is to ensure that the ministry is allocating financial resources efficiently to the areas that the board has designated as important for the health, short-term strategy, and long-term strategy of the ministry. This means that the committee needs to review financial reports, understand sources of income and expenses, know what assets are at the ministry's disposal, understand what liabilities and financial obligations the ministry has, discuss financial policy, review investment portfolio performance, advise staff leadership, and advise the board on policies and executing those policies. This committee should be described and defined in the ministry's bylaws, including defining the number of members the group should have, the committee's officers, any ex officio positions, how many constitutes a quorum, what the committee's responsibilities are, and the committee's relationship to the church's board.

A typical finance committee meeting agenda would consist of a review of the balance sheet and profit loss reports, a discussion of how those look compared to the budget, possibly a discussion about how they compare to the previous year, and discussion about how the remainder of the year looks. If it's late in the year, management would update the board on how the budget is shaping up for the next year. If bank balances are low, they would add a cash flow forecast to the agenda. Other topics might include whether or not to approve capital expenditures or unforeseen significant   expenses, compensation policy and packages, how to invest and use the proceeds of major gifts, how to respond to sudden losses of income, and anything else that is going to have a financial impact on the ministry. Meeting minutes should be taken, submitted to the board for their benefit and decision-making process, and archived in the permanent record of the church.

Because of the finance committee's role, members are typically financially savvy or at least comfortable discussing numbers, are discreet about their discussions, can maintain poise during stressful times, are thoughtful and considerate of the role of finance in a world driven by religious and social good, are able to function independently and without conflict of interest, and are able to clearly articulate their opinions and recommendations.

Speaking from very practical experience, the composition and function of the finance committee at The Parish of Calvary-St. George's where I attend and serve is an excellent model. It is well-rounded in terms of skills and perspectives. We have a person who works in investments, one certified public accountant/tax preparer, one management accountant, two attorneys, and as ex officio members we have the Rector, the church's business manager, and the vestry's treasurer (who also works in investments).

This group meets monthly, for typically an hour, to review year-to-date financials against budget and prior year, to recommend mid-year operating adjustments in order to continue meeting and exceeding net surplus, to review and recommend extraordinary and capital expenditures to the vestry, to review the audit, and to be an additional financial expertise resource to the church. For example, when a long-term tenant moved out of the annex, the properties committee asked our opinion on the best options for using the new space. Our investment oriented members meet with our portfolio manager annually to discuss performance and strategy. I've been working with the preschool director on budgeting and reporting. Our attorney members have been available to help with contracts. These are all ways that the unique talents of various individuals on the committee have supported our church by donating their time and expertise.

How your finance committee looks for your church or ministry is going to depend on who is available to serve. As I mentioned previously, it's a matter of first determining what is needed, then filling it in with the resources you have available. If the resources are there, then all the better. If not, then perhaps you'll need to connect with individuals outside of the church to gain the knowledge, expertise, and perspective on an informal basis.

Questions to ask about the finance committee:
- Does our ministry have a group of people who understand financial reports and discuss the implications of the information for our ministry?
- Do we have a group of people who can hear the vision for our ministry and estimate income and costs associated so that we have a complete picture of the financial impact of our strategy?
- Does this group of people meet formally or informally?
- How often does this group of people review the financial reports?

Visit www.TowerMinistryFinance.com/FreedomToServe to download a sample finance committee agenda and minutes template.

Liability Insurance Broker

One of the most important things we need to do as ministry stewards is to protect the ministry. It's important to understand that ministries become more valuable over time provided they are nurtured properly. As the institution, through its people, becomes more knowledgeable and retains that knowledge through documentation, the staff become more experienced at their jobs, operational structures are established, and the ministry's reputation grows. It is our responsibility to protect this asset.

However, all it takes is one incident to significantly destroy value to the point where the ministry is hurt financially, or even effectively wiped out for that matter. We're aware of the salacious scandals that hit national news, such as Jim Bakker's sex scandal and the subsequent financial fraud discovered at or the questions raised about executive compensation at the United Way. What about the accidents, mistakes, and problems at local nonprofits that don't get reported? Are they any less significant just because they're less exciting or are mere footnotes on the local news? To the people whose lives have been transformed because of those ministries, it doesn't matter the size or scope of the ministry.

The purpose of the liability insurance broker is to provide our ministries with an insurance policy that protects us financially. Here's the beautiful thing about insurance brokers: they have a vested interest in making sure we never have to use insurance, and as such, they are our partners in identifying potential risks to begin with! This means that we can and should ask them what the most common risks are for our specific ministry, ask them to recommend appropriate in-surance coverage, and ask them to guide us to prevent dam-damage from ever occurring.

In general, churches will need to make sure that their build-ings and the contents are insured. For churches, this can prove challenging since the buildings are often old, so be sure to have an inspector perform a valuation or use a valua-tion tool to assist you. Additionally, churches often have artwork, artifacts, rare books, and collectibles. Be sure to keep an inventory of these and have an appraiser value them. Ideally a church would also keep digital photos and a video walk through of the premises that are archived online so that the church has access to them in case the building is damaged beyond repair.

Every ministry should have an umbrella policy, particularly for church events held on or off the property. Also make sure that any organization renting from the church obtains its own liability insurance with the ministry added as an ad-ditional named insured. If the ministry has events outside normal daily activities, such as mission trips or conferences where there is travel, mention them to your broker to see if travel or event policies are needed.

Any organization that does counseling, teaching, or mentor-ing needs to conduct background checks, get references, and get abuse and molestation policies in addition to having strict policies in place about the behavior between adults and children.

We'll discuss protecting ministries later in the book when we look at risk, which is an important yet underrated topic for organizations. In the meantime, be sure to have a good broker on your team. Reach out to other trusted advisors for recommendations, and when meeting a potential broker, make sure that they have experience with religious institutions. Finally, they should be willing to give an initial consultation at no cost to your ministry.

Questions to ask yourself about an insurance broker:
- Do we have someone who understands what our risks are and can effectively explain them to us?
- Will this person be a partner in helping us determine how to prevent negative events from happening?
- Will they shop around for the best coverage at a reasonable cost?

Lawyer

While lawyers are generally not thought of as financial people, their value is also related to risk. A good attorney is going to reduce risk by looking for potential any legal exposure the ministry has to lawsuits, to ensure that the nonprofit is correctly incorporated in its state, to advise in the establishment and amendment of the organization's by-laws, to help the ministry obey civil law, to help prevent problems by reducing exposure through management changes and contractual changes, and by advising and representing the ministry when legal counsel is required.

There are two key aspects to consider when dealing with attorneys. The first is to make sure that the ministry has an attorney who practices law in the area that is needed—the *type* of law. Just as there are different fields of accounting, there are different practice areas in law. Having a church or nonprofit specialist is an obvious choice for ministries, but it might not be enough for your ministry's needs. If you own a property and buildings, you may need a different attorney for dealing with issues related to real estate. Having a persistent problem with a former employee? That would be a labor issue and could require a different lawyer.

The second key aspect when dealing with lawyers is that there are different legal jurisdictions throughout the United States. There's federal law, state law, and local laws, which effectively creates several layers of laws that need to be taken into consideration. The simplest way to look at it is to understand that *state* bar associations certify attorneys via the bar exam, and therefore we need to look for an attorney who is authorized to practice in the state in question.

As you work with your attorney, identify best practices and legal documents you need on a regular basis. This will appear costly, but when amortized over the years you'll use this information, it is a worthwhile investment. Additionally, not everything needs to be done at once. Sit down with an attorney and explain what it is you are trying to achieve, and they will tell you what you'll need and when you need it.

It is very important to keep your attorney aware of what you're doing before you do it. In my own financial work, I see problems that could easily have been avoided had the client written or called to simply inform me as to their intent and goals, and likewise, many attorneys experience similar issues. Be sure to make a quick phone call or send a quick note to explain new initiatives with a request to inform you of any yellow or red flags.

How does a ministry find a good lawyer? As with searching for any service professional, ask for referrals. Put out feelers through your network of other clergy, ministries, and non-profit professionals in the community. When it comes to the law, ministries have an additional tool available: the Christian Legal Society. This association of legal professionals includes attorneys, judges, law students, and law firm professionals and has a legal referral service on their web site to help find an attorney that is right for your ministry. In addition to searching by state, one may also look under law practice areas including non-profit organization law, church law, and employment law.

Questions to ask about an attorney:

- Do we have general counsel we can go to for legal advice as needed?
- Are we doing our part to include this counsel as we plan and think about what our strategies and associated risks are?
- Does this person have contacts in the legal community who can step in as legal specialists if needed?

Banker

Perhaps it is because I live in a large city that seems devoid of good relationship banking, or perhaps it really is a nationwide issue: it seems these days with Internet and phone banking that there is less need for having a relationship with an individual at the bank. However, what I have found from days past when I knew my banker was that they are invaluable when you need information or have an urgent need. It is my advice to do what you can to make a personal contact with a local bank.

Also, thanks to our modern ability to conduct business with organizations remotely, I recommend looking into financial institutions that specifically serve churches and ministries. Because they work specifically with similar organizations, they are more likely to understand and be sympathetic to our needs. For example, most for-profit banks will not lend money unless they can look at tax returns or have physical assets that act as collateral against the loan. This is especially challenging for churches that do not need to even need to prepare an exempt organization tax return, and can even be daunting for ministries that don't have assets.

Finally, consider having multiple bank accounts to play each financial institution off each other. I had one client that was looking for a line of credit, and they were able to approach two different institutions they had relationships with and were successful with one but not the other. So consider keeping two accounts in two different banks; one for an operating account and the other for a reserve account, thereby establishing an additional relationship and history that could be helpful later on.

Questions to ask about the banker:
- Do we have someone at our bank who reviews our account at least once annually to ensure that we have the best type of account for our needs?
- If we need a loan, do we have an individual we can approach to discuss our ministry vision, what type of loan we need, and the amount we are looking for?

Investment Advisor

If your ministry has a lot of money in reserves—enough to cover at least six months' of expenses, if there is a significant bequest, or if there is an endowment, then the ministry should put the money into investments.

There are five issues to consider when investing: what the ministry needs the investment funds for, what the time horizon is for the funds, the organization's tolerance for risk, how much return the ministry wants on the investment, and what the purpose of the principle and financial return will be used for. This is going to significantly vary depending on the organization and the circumstances in which it finds itself. However, nonprofits are correctly viewed as needing to protect funds more than grow, so it's best to find ways to invest that are low risk while maintaining better returns than what banks typically offer.

This leads us to the question: who is the right type of person to be an investment advisor? This too is going to vary depending on the organization and circumstances. For small organizations with little to invest, it may be an individual or group of individuals volunteering their time and expertise. A smaller ministry might shop around for an investment firm that manages its portfolio for them. Large ministries may reach a point where they have full-time staff dedicated to monitoring and managing the investment portfolio.

Given that the vast majority of churches and ministries aren't in the position to have staff and volunteers manage investments, there are some characteristics to look for when choosing an investment firm. First, find someone with a good track record working with churches and ministries, or at least nonprofits in general. Second, as part of that track record, make sure that they can and will invest in stocks that are aligned with the ministry's moral principles. Third, make sure that they offer a discounted fee structure. Finally, they need to track against benchmarks to make sure that you're getting results you need.

Regardless of who advises the ministry on investments, it is especially important to remember that the investment advisor is an agent. Sometimes agents are great, and sometimes they are terrible. When it comes to investing, make sure that your investment advisor cannot access money for their own purposes, that they do not charge for trades (which leads to the practice of frequently buying and selling stock for the sole purpose of increasing their fees—commonly known as churning), that the investment account is audited annually, and they have clear direction for what their role and responsibilities are.

Questions to ask about the investment advisor:
- Do we have enough money to start investing? If not, how soon can we begin?
- What type of investment advisor do we need? Are we in the position to have a professional advisor or should we use a person or committee?
- Is our investment advisor a good agent and will they always act in our ministry's best interest?
- Have we done our part to define the outcomes we want from our investment and communicate our guidelines to the investment advisor?

Certified Public Accountant

After the lengthy commentary on the necessity of a management accountant and the frustrations of reports prepared by certified public accountants (CPAs), one might think that a CPA would be of no value to a ministry. However, this is not the case for two reasons.

First, CPAs are trained and tested on financial disciplines that are very valuable to organizations of any size. They ask important questions about what controls are in place to prevent fraud. They can help bring structure and order to situations where none currently exist. They are advisors for additional perspectives on difficult and complex financial questions, and they are the go-to people for understanding nonprofit tax issues.

This last point is particularly important. Just because nonprofit organizations don't pay income taxes the way businesses are required doesn't mean there aren't taxes to consider. There are plenty of other taxes that permeate God's business! With even one employee, there are payroll taxes to deal with. If you sell books or recordings, there are likely sales taxes. If you run a for-profit business under your non-profit to raise money, you'll likely need to report unrelated business tax. Contributions have tax implications for the ministry and the donor. Expenses need to comply with tax law by being legitimate ministry expenses under IRS Code. For example, a spouse's meal while dining out with donors cannot be expensed by the nonprofit. Unless the spouse is an integral part of the ministry, their meal is not considered a ministry expense.

The second reason why a CPA is invaluable is because every non-church ministry must comply with federal law by preparing and filing an annual IRS form 990 to maintain its charitable status. This is not an option. Even my Toastmasters club needs to submit a form 990-N, which is a simplified form of the form 990 for the smallest of nonprofits.

If your ministry receives between $50,000 and $200,000 in receipts, a form 990-EZ needs to be filed. If your receipts are less, then the IRS only requires a postcard to ensure their records are updated, which is what my Toastmasters club does. If $200,000 or more, then a full-blown form 990 needs to be filed, and since IRS instructions make the King James Version of the Bible sound like Dr. Seuss, you'd be much better offloading the responsibility to a local certified public accounting firm.

There may also be state charity filing requirements in your state. Nonprofits in New York are registered with the Attorney General's Charities Bureau and are required to submit annual reports. Charities across the river in New Jersey are registered with the Charitable Registration & Investigation Section, which is a part of the New Jersey Division of Consumer Affairs. They too must file an annual report. Across the Long Island Sound, nonprofits must register with the Connecticut Department of Consumer Protection annually.

How do we find a good certified public accountant? Like any other professional service search, it's a combination of finding out who is available through research, asking peers and friends for recommendations, and asking the right questions. Unless a firm has a history of audit violations, I would be less concerned about how a firm conducts its audits and technical ability. Instead, look for fit: how much work they do with nonprofits, what size of organizations they typically work with, and if their personality fits the ministry's culture.

Questions to ask about a certified public accountant:
- Do we need a certified public accountant for tax or regulatory issues?
- Do we have someone to go to who can answer questions about tax and accounting laws?
- Does this person understand accounting rules as they apply to nonprofits and churches?

Clergy / Personal Tax Advisor

Thinking back to the previous section on payroll systems, we recall that there are three parties involved in the payroll transaction: the employer, the employee, and the government, which is really a number of agencies. Without taxes the transaction is purely between the employer and the employee. As previously discussed though, the employer needs to fulfill its responsibility as a tax collection agent for the government since taxes are added to the transaction. What is not the employer's responsibility is being a tax advisor to its employees. It is the employee's responsibility to understand their tax obligations, to correctly estimate their annual tax bill, and to convey to the employer what withholdings they want to have.

So why then do I recommend a personal tax preparer as a resource for the organization? For several reasons.

The first is that a personal tax preparer is another tax resource beyond the certified public accountant and may offer perspectives that the CPA cannot. For example, as a personal tax preparer, they will likely have a heightened sense about what qualifies as a charitable contribution. After all, part of their business is to make sure that their clients don't overpay taxes, so they need to know what constitutes a charitable deduction.

Second, a personal tax preparer can help your ministry's finance staff confirm withholding tax amounts. When a client's staff comes to me with questions about their withholdings, I'll typically be able to answer the question with the caveat that that I'm not a professional tax preparer and that they should speak with an outside tax advisor. At that point, we'll go to a tax specialist for their expertise. This route mitigates risk to the organization without coming across as being difficult to work with on taxes. The result is that the employee gets the knowledge they need to correctly set their withholding while the ministry removes itself from appearing like a tax advisor. If the ministry appears to have offered tax advice, then it puts itself at risk if the employee has tax problems and is looking for someone to blame.

The last reason to have a personal tax preparer available is that it helps care for employees. Incorrect tax treatment of any worker, but especially of clergy, puts both the individual and the ministry at risk. One of my clients brings a clergy tax specialist in at the beginning of every year for employees (of whom many are simply not tax savvy) to estimate their annual tax expenses and set up their withholdings. Since we began this practice, the number of mid-year adjustments and crises has noticeably decreased, much to everyone's satisfaction.

Finding a good tax consultant, especially for clergy, is difficult, but it is not impossible. Be sure to ask anyone you're considering what type of clients they typically work with and if they have experience working with nonprofit employees or in churches. Also find out what their billing structure is like (hourly, annual retainer, quarterly retainer) and what it covers (only tax preparation, responding to Internal Revenue Service notices) and what it doesn't cover.

Questions to ask about your clergy / personal tax preparer:

- Do we have an individual income tax specialist our clergy can contact when they have questions about their taxes?
- Does this individual understand income taxes as applied to clergy, including the implications of clergy housing deductions and other ministry-related deductions?
- Is this person also available to staff for general tax questions?

Human Resources Consultant

Having personnel gives ministries the ability to create an organization that creates an even greater impact on the local community. This truly is a wonderful thing. When a small ministry has impact, donors see the good it is doing, funds come in, the team grows, and impact increases. The additional staff provides relief to the original team because management will be able to delegate tasks that are less value-added, in turn allowing executives to focus on high-impact tasks and strategy. Additional skilled staff will bring specialized talent to the ministry that it had limited access to before. Further, an excellent team provides relationships that encourage and nurture us. We end up with a "family away from family" who know us, care about us, and share in our joys and pains. That's the upside of working with others.

The downside is that bad relationships can become weeds in the modern garden of work, increasing the toil and labor that God told Adam of after the Fall. Our organizations are filled with sinners whose personalities are tainted, who come to work after a difficult time with family or a rough commute, and there they collide others with similar problems. The air can become filled with miscommunications and misunderstandings, and on top of *that*, our governments have written volumes upon volumes of text about hiring and business practices that we really aren't concerned about. Why can't we all just get along, do some ministry, and go home satisfied that we've been worthy servants at the end of the day?

This is where a human resources professional is helpful. First, they are available to explain the basics of the law and boil those volumes down into a summary that we can be mindful of as we manage our human resource functions. Second, they can tell us what practices we need to follow in the ministry—what we need to do and when to execute these tasks. Annual reviews, protocols to follow in case of conflicts, what to do in case of injury, and how to address accusations are just some of the things we must be prepared to handle. Third, they can provide us with the templates needed as we grow the ministry. This would include recruiting templates, annual review forms, paid time off documents, etc.

Finally, they need to be a resource whenever something arises. Just like we should tell our lawyers when we are planning something new or there's an incident that could lead to a lawsuit, we need to inform the human resources consultant that we're hiring for a new position, that an employee is leaving, or that a conflict has escalated between a key executive and their assistant. It doesn't need to be a formal notification, and it doesn't need to be lengthy. A simple e-mail or message to say that something is going on will be enough to get a good HR consultant thinking about what should be done and which pitfalls to look out for and discuss with you. This small investment in time could save the ministry hours of headache and a lot of money.

Questions to ask about an HR consultant:

- Do we have someone who advises us on the latest personnel regulations?
- When we have a significant personnel matter—new hire, departure, or personnel conflict—do we have someone who will guide us through both legal and human relations aspects so that we have a greater chance of a satisfactory outcome?

Benefits and Retirement Advisors

Finally, it helps to have benefits consultants to guide the ministry through the appropriate types of benefits available to the ministry and staff. There are really two key reasons to have benefits: it saves the ministry money courtesy of payroll tax deductions, and because they increase the value of compensation packages through employees' tax savings.

A benefits consultant will help in the benefits selection process, and they should be knowledgeable about government mandated policies, such as disability and insurance policy. Depending on circumstances, you may need different consultants for different insurances.

Additionally, part of our prudence and stewardship as individuals is to be prepared for our well-being after active ministry, so a retirement specialist can guide us through our options. This is especially important for ministers who qualify for housing allowance, because *the right retirement plan will have a feature that exempts the housing allowance component of future payouts from income tax*. Yes, you read that right. All contributions are exempt from taxes at the time of contribution, but future withdrawals will be taxed unless a housing allowance is specified. That will still be exempt. In fact, I had one church client that had already begun the paperwork for a non-clergy specific retirement plan but stopped after I intervened. We then spoke to someone who could set up a clergy-type plan. Estimated tax savings? $80,000 so far.

Even if the ministry is not ready to establish benefit plans, the discussions should start so those in leadership roles can plan for the time when they can begin. This brings a tremendous value to the staff and to the ministry. So what should a ministry look for in a retirement planner? First, check the credentials. A Certified Financial Planner© (CFP) has been through robust training and testing, and they have met experiential requirements. Second, make sure that you are working with someone who is a good agent—someone who will look out for your well-being. Third, this should be someone you and your staff can be completely comfortable and open with about your respective goals and desires.

Questions to ask about a benefits consultants and retirement specialists:

- Do we have someone to go to who can tell us what our legal obligations are to our employees?
- Can we discuss our staff and what their non-salary compensation needs and wants are?
- Does this person know what is available in the marketplace, and will they be able to make suitable recommendations to us?
- Is now an appropriate time in the life of our ministry to start a retirement plan?
- Do we have a retirement specialist that we've discussed retirement plans with?
- Is this person familiar with the type of plan ministries and clergy should have?

NOTES

NOTES

_____

_____

_____

_____

_____

_____

_____

_____

_____

_____

_____

_____

_____

How

Now that we've talked about the *what* and *who* of financial ministry, we are ready to talk about *how* we need to execute it properly. It's not enough to have tools, materials, and construction workers on site at the building going up on my street. The workers need direction on how to assemble those materials to create the building to code. So they have blueprints, plumbing diagrams, and electrical diagrams that the foreman reads with them so that they work together to finish the job correctly.

In this section we are going to look at the following areas that define *how* we do things:

- Policies
- Procedures
- Controls
- Risk
- Integrations
- Accounting Entries
- Financial Hygiene
- Close Process

As with the other sections, there's a reason to the order of these topics. Policies need to be defined first because they dictate everything else that happens in the organization. Then we look at procedures—how we carry out the policies that the board stipulates. Following the procedures is a discussion on financial controls; they are a key aspect of procedures that we need to be mindful of as we outline financial processes. Another key aspect of procedures is risk, so we add that in next. Then we will think about how our different financial components need to be integrated so that they work well together. We'll also look at accounting entries to understand what our financial team does and how it needs to execute their tasks. We'll take a look a financial hygiene and the healthy financial management habits we need in order to fulfill our roles as ministry managers, and finally, we'll look at a key area of financial hygiene: the monthly close process.

Of everything written in this book, explaining how to do things is the most difficult. Every organization will have different policies based on the board's and management's views on its mission, ministry philosophy, operating philosophy, and the way it conducts business. For example, in my work with churches I have never had two churches with the same financial report formats. Not even once.

Still, I'm including a discussion on how to do things in spite of this difficulty for two reasons. First, this will act as a checklist by which you can compare what "hows" you need to what your ministry currently has. Second, I want to stimulate your thinking about how you can manage the process of filling in the gaps. After all, just because you have all the components doesn't mean that they'll work right—you need to make sure that everything works together properly to serve your ministry.

Policies

From the very top level, policies guide how a ministry functions. In short, the board needs to sit down and say, "This is our mission, and this is how we are going to do business to fulfill that mission." The board members are especially important since they inform how things are done throughout the organization. For example, a policy of creating a safe environment for children will affect processes for hiring youth workers, counseling teens, and background checks for certain paid and volunteer positions in the church. So policy needs to be determined *before* process can be defined.

Many organizations follow the practice of creating a policy and procedure manual to codify their policies and operations. Perhaps I'm being a bit contrarian, but I advise my clients to create a policy book separately from the procedure book for both philosophical and practical reasons. The philosophical reason is that the board needs to focus on policy and only on policy. There's no specific reason for a board to delve into procedures, which are the day-to-day management and execution of financial tasks. Practically speaking, keeping policies separate from the procedure manual means that the board has a pithy document devoid of information it would consider useless. So when the board or a committee needs to check on the status of a policy, they don't have a lengthy manual to consult. Simply look for the page with the current policy, and it is right there, absent the staff's notes on how this impacts their work.

Finally, a policy doesn't need to be long nor does it need to be complicated. For example, a check signing policy could be, "Checks may be signed by anyone authorized, provided that the check is not made out to them for payroll or reimbursement. Two signatures are required if the check amount is $2,500 or greater." Nothing fancy, but it gets the point across.

Some of the financial policies your ministry might consider are:
- Accounting method (cash or accrual)
- Depreciation method and fixed asset parameters, including the minimum threshold for capitalizing and what depreciation method is utilized
- Budget preparation, approval, and changes
- Conflicts of interest
- Gift acceptance policy
- Expense reimbursement policy
- Check signing authorizations
- Accruals: what to accrue, what is the minimum threshold for accruing, and how is this calculated
- Revenue recognition
- Finance committee composition and meeting frequency
- Investments
- Spending limits by job position

Questions to ask about policies:

- Has our board taken the time to specify our policies—what our ministry needs and what must be prevented?
- Has someone taken the time to document those policies?
- Are those policies part of our legal records?
- Do people in positions of authority—paid and lay—know what those policies are? Have they signed off that they agree to those policies, and are they following and enforcing them?

Visit www.TowerMinistryFinance.com/FreedomToServe for sample policies.

Procedures

Once policies have been established, we can move into detailing how we are going to perform job functions. This really should take place across the organization. By documenting the steps each person takes to complete a routine job, the ministry will have institutional knowledge, will ensure that the function can be completed when the individual is on vacation, will be sure that there are smooth transitions when employees transition out of their roles, and ensures that infrequently executed processes will be completed correctly.

I'm a huge believer in mapping and outlining processes because establishing it correctly from the beginning allows ministries to delegate as much as possible to junior staff who can take care of administrative overhead at a much lesser cost. In my consulting practice, I will work with organizations to identify what needs to be done, talk through the process with their staff, and then either outline it for them or even go so far as to create a video tutorial if software is involved.

Financial procedures come in three flavors. First, there are processes that might be viewed ancillary to finance: employee processes such as recruiting and onboarding come to mind, as well as routines in place to mitigate risk, such as doing an annual review with the liability insurance broker or making sure that all contractors have completed contracts and submitted W-9 forms for IRS compliance. Second, there are processes related to *executing* financial transactions, offering count procedures, approving and paying bills, and preparing payroll are all types of procedures that need to be thought out. Finally, there are processes for *recording* financial entries: how we record offering, enter bills, and input payroll are all processes of their own.

You might be asking yourself how detailed these procedures should be and even how detailed the documentation needs to be. As with many answers in this book, this will vary for each organization since each has unique needs and perspectives. However, in principle, it helps to think on two levels: accuracy and ease. If the task doesn't require significant accuracy, then it won't be complex and the instructions can be general. If it needs to be completed to exact specifications, then the process will be highly defined and the instructions very detailed and clear. After that, we should worry about getting the job done as quickly and as cheaply as possible.

Questions about procedures:
- Have we listed every activity that we execute and outlined what steps are required to complete those activities?
- If not, why not?
- If so:
  o Have we tested them by asking staff to follow them to see whether or not they are accurate?
  o Where do we keep these? Do all affected staff and volunteers know where to find them?
  o When is the last time they were updated?
  o Have we made it clear to employees that failure to follow the procedures could affect their performance reviews?

Visit www.TowerMinistryFinance.com/FreedomToServe for sample procedures.

Controls

A key part of processes are controls. These are steps put in place to ensure that the desired results are achieved. For example, insisting that youth ministers have certain educational requirements, have background checks, that your church contact their prior employers to verify qualifications, and checking that there have been no hints of improprieties are all controls towards ensuring a positive environment for teens and apply to our need to mitigate risk to children and our ministry. Likewise, rotating offering ushers, having two different counters, creating tally sheets that the counters complete and sign, putting the offering, lock bag, and depositing in a safe are examples of controls required to ensure that what the church receives actually makes it to the bank.

Some of the financial controls you may need include:
- Collecting and counting offerings
- Online banking access
- Petty cash access and accounting
- Check access
- Printing and signing checks (including double signatures for larger checks)
- Credit card limits and authorizations
- Payroll time sheet approval and submission
- Bank reconciliation
- Access to confidential documents

As you think about controls and what you need for your ministry, there are a few different mindsets to take.

First, as you look at the list of things that your team does financially, such as receiving money, spending money, buying food supplies, and ordering medicines for third world countries, think about, "How could we lose money through fraud or error?" Chances are the process for doing anything is linear, and by looking at the process on paper, you'll be able to think about where weaknesses may be present. If your ministry has a process for ordering and distributing medicine, you can see on your process where there would be plenty of areas for medicine to be stolen from the ministry: the order amount might be inflated so that the excess might be stolen, the amount received might be less than the amount ordered, or the amount distributed might be less than the amount received.

Second, while a lot of the focus on controls deals with preventing fraud, it can and should be expanded to think about ensuring a predictable outcome. Thinking back to our discussion on investments, I mentioned that a ministry will want to determine what sort of return it gets on investment given its tolerance for a given level of risk. That expected return is a predictable outcome. If it doesn't achieve that return then something went wrong along the way, and the ministry will want to review what happened. Was it an anomaly—a bad month—or is the investment manager not performing to expectations? Maybe there really is fraud. You can see how controls are about assuring outcome. The reason fraud shows up is that control failures can easily lead to fraud, which left unfettered could become significant losses.

Third, be mindful of the differences between preventative (front-end) and detective (back-end controls). Preventative controls stop the problem from occurring in the first place. Due diligence on hiring is a perfect example of a front-end control. So is establishing spending limits on credit cards up front. Detective controls might include allowing members of the youth group to give feedback of a youth minister's performance review, comparing spending to budget to confirm the ministry hasn't overspent, or counting medicine inventory to confirm it matches records. By having preventative and detective controls, the organization has a greater chance of eliminating problems to begin with. In fact, merely having and practicing good controls acts as deterrents because staff and volunteers are aware that they are being monitored.

Finally, one of the best and easiest controls are to make sure that more than one person is involved in the process. Splitting up the labor of a job is an excellent way of making sure that staff are watching and watching out for each other. Even with simple cases of, "Did X get done?", having other people aware of the job at hand helps ensure that the steps are remembered and the job completed.

Questions to ask about controls:
- Have you reviewed your processes and asked, "What could go wrong?"
- Have you added steps to prevent bad outcomes from occurring?
- Have you put steps at the end to check outcomes and to correct bad outcomes?

Risk

An often overlooked aspect of our responsibility for ministries is protecting ourselves from loss. In some ways accidents are events that are failures in control—either because the control was weak and failed to prevent the event, because the circumstances leading up to the event were not foreseen, or simply because the event could not be prevented.

Loss can occur in many forms: financial loss from a parishioner injured on a slippery sidewalk, reputation loss due to scandal, failure to gain a major contribution due to staff negligence to follow through with the donor, financial repercussion from a copyright lawsuit... and the list goes on. The bottom line is that there are many risks around us, and as stewards of the ministry, we are charged with the responsibility of protecting the ministry entrusted to our care.

When it comes to risk there are three principles we should be mindful of. First, think about what could go wrong. Just like the, "Where could we lose money?" question under controls, we need to think about where the ministry is vulnerable to potential problems that could become even larger issues.

Second, think about these different scenarios by asking two questions: "What is the likelihood that this scenario could actually happen?" and "What is the potential damage if this actually happened?" Answering these questions is going to give us a sense of what is important. I'm not going to address the risk of stubbing my toe (happens all the time but with little impact), nor will I plan for a plane crashing into my house (unlikely and not much I can do about it), but I will think about the risk of a fire in my kitchen (high enough likelihood and could be a real disaster).

Third, with these things in mind, there are four questions to ask: 1) How do we prevent this scenario from happening in the first place?, 2) If it happens, how do we mitigate the damage?, 3) How do we recover from such an event?, and 4) What insurance do we need to make up for the anticipated financial loss that we would have to pay for recovery and the restitution owed? These questions are especially important in light of the previous discussion about liability insurance brokers. *We don't want problems to occur in the first place, and the process for prevention starts here.* The beautiful thing is that this is a one-time exercise that helps protect the organization for life, with some updates as the ministry and times change.

So how would this process look like within the setting of a church? Let's take my kitchen example and apply it to a parish fellowship hall's kitchen. What could possibly go wrong? We've already established that there could be a fire, but someone might slip on a spill, fall, and hurt themselves, or someone might cut themselves while prepping a meal. So there are three scenarios we want to address in our risk plan. For now, let's focus on the fire, which we need to prevent, mitigate, recover, and insure.

To *prevent* the fire from occurring, the church has established protocols to make sure that unnecessary flammable materials are restricted from the kitchen, that volunteers cannot wear loose clothing, and that staff and volunteers are trained on safe cooking procedures. These rules are written and posted so that anyone walking into the kitchen can see them.

In the event a fire does break out, the church has the following steps to mitigate the risk: a) fire extinguishers are provided next to the stove and at the kitchen door, b) a sprinkler system has been installed, c) the staff checks the extinguisher on a monthly basis to measure pressure and other concerns, d) the sprinkler system is inspected annually, e) staff are trained on what to do when a fire breaks out, and f) instructions are also posted in the kitchen on a clip board so that they can be removed when staff evacuate the premises.

While the church hopes that there will never be a fire, it has already determined that, if there is a fire, after-service fellowship would take place in a different area of the church, and the weekly soup kitchen operations would continue down the street at another church.

Lastly, the insurance agent recommended that the facility be insured for $2 million based on the estimate to rebuild the facility. This estimate is reviewed annually and the insurance coverage increased accordingly.

As with many other exercises in this book, the level of detail depends on the sophistication of your ministry. One of my church clients had about 40 different scenarios that we worked on together, including children's ministry, risk scenarios traveling to / from / and at retreats, violent crime carried out at a worship service, and copyright infringement, among many others. It sounds like a lot of work, but it does not have to be. Having meetings with the right people and asking, "What could go wrong and what can we do about it?" is a much better approach than nothing at all. It's a one-time project that needs to be maintained and implemented once completed.

Questions to ask about risk:
- Have we identified areas of the ministry where we could be sued?
- Have we identified areas of ministry where we could experience fraud?
- Have we identified areas of the ministry where someone could be physically or emotionally injured?
- Have we identified areas of the ministry where we could lose money or property?
- What steps have we taken or plan to take in order to prevent such events from occurring?
- Do we have, or will we have in the near future, a document available to staff and volunteers to explain our ways of avoiding negative events and dealing with them if they do occur?
- Have we discussed these with our liability insurance broker?

Visit www.TowerMinistryFinance.com/FreedomToServe for sample risk procedures.

Accounting Software Configuration

Earlier in the book I mentioned that the primary purpose of the accounting software is to collect and consolidate transaction data to create reports for the board so they can make strategic decisions. In daily ministry, it works as follows: every day staff are making transactions—collecting and depositing money, buying supplies, running payroll, having coffee with volunteers, looking for and buying vacation Bible school materials, replenishing the pantry for the soup kitchen, etc. However, it can be hard for us to make decisions on individual transactions. It's when we look at the aggregate of the accumulated purchases that we begin to see the clear picture of overspending in one area and understand underinvestment in another. As such, we need a tool that collects these little pieces of information and lets us summarize them in categories and time periods that we define. Certainly the details are available to look at, but the value is truly in being able to consolidate a lot of information and let us "see the forest" and not just the trees. Once we see the forest, we can see areas where there are problems—ones that we might not see in just one or two transactions—and address them.

Understanding what our goal is—aggregating and reporting on information—we now understand our approach to how we go about setting up and using our accounting software. It depends on how the ministry understands its income and expenses, and how it itemizes and consolidates information. This can and will be different for every ministry. An Assemblies of God church plant will have different activities and needs than a 150-year-old Episcopal church, and their respective ministers and boards have different perspectives on financials. Likewise, a 150-year-old Episcopal church will probably have different requirements than the 100-year-old Episcopal Church 5 miles away is experiencing an influx of immigrants. Even the 150-year-old church could be a different church in 10 years when the current rector retires and a new, younger rector steps in with new perspectives!

It is very important to define how the financials need to look before setting up the general ledger software. This is one of the first things I typically discuss with a client. If it's a new church with no accounting software, we start from scratch. If it's an established church or ministry, we typically move information around so that it is organized to our purposes.

In principle, I recommend two levels of detail. The first level is the "big buckets" of information to cover the major areas that we're summarizing: payroll costs, Christian education, worship expenses, evangelism supplies, or community outreach can be considered big buckets. Within those big buckets is the second level—the little buckets.[2]

A community outreach bucket might have delivery van rental, contract labor, food supplies, and personal hygiene

---

[2] There are a number of different analogies that can be used here. During training with a church's staff I was told by a group of women that they should be looked at as mother / child relationships! You can use whatever analogy suits you best, provided you understand that there are ways of seeing consolidated information and then be expanding to see further details.

supplies for the homeless. Evangelism expenses might include travel expenses, Bibles and track, and volunteer training. Within your travel expenses, we might have additional buckets (in accounting terms, these buckets are called accounts) for guest speakers, facility rental, refreshments, and volunteer training. So we can keep additional levels if we want. However, at some point we reach the level of specificity that doesn't make sense—it's so detailed that the purpose of summarizing information no longer applies.

Now these are primarily focused on the profit and loss / statement of activity reports. This is not to say that the balance sheet is less important. It is very important! I generally find that a board will focus more on the statement of activity against budget to make financial decisions. The statement of activity can also be the lengthier report to review, so its configuration has greater impact on how boards understand or are befuddled by the information contained in it.

Finally, this should be done under the guidance of a management accountant who has experience creating financial reports for business owners and executives. We certainly want to create a financial structure appropriate to the ministry, but within the rules and best practices of professional accounting.

Questions to ask about how to set up the accounting software:

- From a high level, how do we segment the major areas of our ministry?
- If we look at a balance sheet report, can we understand our assets, liabilities, and overall financial position?
- When we look at a profit and loss statement, can we quickly see how well or poorly we are doing?

Visit www.TowerMinistryFinance.com/FreedomToServe to see a variety of report configurations in summary and detail as well as contrasted among different types of churches.

Accounting Entries

Once the accounting software is set up and ready for use, the finance staff can begin using it on a daily basis. How they add entries into the accounting software is going to depend on what software is being used, what integrations are available, and what controls have been established.

The approach that I recommend to my clients is to make a list of the different types of entries (contributions via check, contributions via credit card, check payments, payroll, etc.), look at that list alongside a financial report, determine how the information gets consolidated into that report, and then document how each entry needs to be made in the accounting software. This is yet another situation where having expert help is going to improve efficiency. Most people aren't trained to make the connection between the "upstream" entry and the "downstream" report the way that accountants are, and this is where it pays to have an expert work with you to take your reports, look at the software's features, and map out data entry processes.

I should mention that there are two types of ways to get information into the accounting software. The first is the most obvious: someone types it in. The second comes to us courtesy of technology that mentioned earlier in the book: integrations allow us to import transaction data from various sources, including the donor software, the payroll service, the credit card company, and the bank. Regardless of *how* transactions are entered, they must be entered. So as you link your different financial components together, you should be mindful that some entries will come courtesy of another component.

Finally, once these accounting entry processes have been established, we can go to the procedure manual and update it with the process for making each entry.

Questions to ask about accounting entries:
- Are our transactions summarized in the right places on our financial reports?
- Have we mapped out all of the entry types in our accounting procedures manual?
- Does everyone on our financial team know the process outlined in the procedures manual?
- Are all staff members following the procedures we established? If not, do procedures need to be revised or does the staff need to be reminded to follow protocol?

Financial Hygiene

As we approach the end our time together in this book, we need to talk about financial hygiene. This is not about scrubbing coins or washing behind presidential ears on paper currency! Rather, this is about our financial routines and habits. Our financial work is of little use if we don't take the time and effort to review it, understand what it is telling us, and taking actions based on the information. You, your bookkeeper, your financial leadership, your finance committee, and your board should all have tasks that each of you do, such as regular check-ins with different members of your internal / external team and reports that you all read as part of your ministry management.

Financial hygiene is not just for large organizations either. I still remember watching my niece and nephews clumsily push toothbrushes against their teeth and chew on bristles when they were toddlers. Sure, it wasn't the right technique, but these were healthy habits that they are carrying with them as they mature into adults. So the sooner we establish financial habits appropriate to where the ministry is at now, the better.

I recommend at least the following:

Daily:
- Check the bank balance, review details to see what the bank processed, and look for potential fraudulent transactions
- Check the credit card for the same criteria
- Bookkeeper processes all transactions

Weekly:
- Confirm with the bookkeeper that all accounts are up to date
- Review the balance sheet, confirm sufficient cash in hand for the next several weeks
- Review a month to date profit and loss report to see how the month is shaping up
- Review bills, make payments

Monthly:
- Close the books
- Review the balance sheet, note working capital (cash + current assets — current liabilities), and confirm it is enough for the next month
- Review the month's profit and loss, check for reasonableness and errors
- Compare year to date profit and loss against the year's *budget*; note significant variances and determine if they indicate changes in the ministry environment that call for strategy change
- Compare year to date profit and loss against last year's profit and loss for the same months; note significant variances and determine if they indicate changes in the ministry environment that call for strategy change
- Confirm all payroll taxes have been paid
- Issue reports to the finance committee

Quarterly:
- Close the books
- Issue reports to the finance committee and the board with any notes about potential changes in the ministry environment that call for strategy change
- Update the financial projection for the year
- Prepare a cash flow forecast for the coming quarter
- File quarterly tax returns

As with many other things, this is going to vary depending on how complex your ministry is, how large it is, and how it conducts God's business. These are provided to stimulate your thinking about what needs to be done. And it must be done! Ignorance is not bliss when it comes to finance. Figure out what needs to be done so that you can start your ministry's financial hygiene and schedule.

Questions to ask yourself and your team about financial hygiene:
- Do we have good habits we engage in to make sure that we're doing well financially?
- Have we made a list of those habits?
- Do we have a calendar or checklist for when we're supposed to do those activities?

Close Process

One element of financial hygiene merits special attention, and that is the period close process. This is the time when all accounts are reconciled, the balance sheet verified, and the profit and loss report checked for accuracy. How frequently this is done depends on the organization.

I recommend handling this task on a quarterly basis at minimum, but it would preferably be a monthly task. The reason for a monthly close is quite practical: when questions inevitably come up about transactions, it is much easier to recall circumstances several weeks ago as opposed to several months ago.

A close is typically completed around 15 days after a month is finished. During the first week or so the bookkeeper finishes their entries, performs any reconciliations they are authorized to perform, and reviews their own work. Then the management accountant or CFO steps into the process to handle reconciliations they need to do. This might include bank account reconciliations, credit card reconciliations, as well as preparing schedules that confirm balances on the balance sheet. Then the management accountant or CFO does analysis on the numbers and highlights trends in performance against budget. Reports with their commentary are issued to senior ministry staff and the finance committee.

There are several benefits to a close process. For one, this routine ensures that the bookkeeping staff maintain a regular rhythm and stay on top of their work. Knowing that they have a deadline will keep this pace going. Second, we all have a tendency to perform better with accountability, and knowing that their numbers will be reviewed in a few short weeks will keep the staff focused on accuracy. Finally, this process ensures that senior management and the board regularly receive current and accurate information they need to guide the ministry.

One of the best things I've done for my nonprofit clients is to insist on regularly closing the books. I delayed implementing it for a long time, worried that clients would view closes as wasted time and money. Instead, we realized that the return on investment is high. The benefit far outweighs the marginal cost of developing and implementing process. Financial reports are being delivered faster with fewer surprises, and more time is spent on making strategic decisions about how to guide the ministry forward.

Questions to ask yourself about the close process:
- How do I know that the numbers I'm looking at on financial reports are correct?
- How often does a financial expert review the bookkeeper's work to check for accuracy?
- Do we have a checklist of things that need to be reviewed to ensure accuracy?
- Do we have a regular date by which financial reports are issued?
- Are ministry managers and the board reviewing those reports and responding by adjusting strategy and activities to reflect what is really happening in the ministry?

Visit www.TowerMinistryFinance.com/FreedomToServe to see a sample close checklist.

NOTES

_____

_____

_____

_____

_____

_____

_____

_____

_____

_____

_____

_____

NOTES

_____

_____

_____

_____

_____

_____

_____

_____

_____

_____

_____

EXECUTION

We've looked at what we need, we've looked at who we need, and now we've considered how we need to do it to the extent that a book can guide these steps. The next question is one of action: "*What is the next step?*" What action, even the simplest of steps, can you take now that will have a significant impact on your ministry?

- ❖ **What** do you need to add or replace in your financial components?
- ❖ **Who** do you need to add or change on your team?
- ❖ Is it clear on **how** finances work in your ministry?

Now, there's a part of me that is concerned that you might be thinking that your ministry is not the right size for some of these recommendations, that the time is not right, or that there is some other "not right" issue that's preventing your ministry from moving forward. I truly understand that this happens. There's only so much time in a day and so many other priorities. However, speaking for myself, there are numerous projects and habits that I should have implemented earlier in my life that would have made a bigger difference today. So please, don't let some "not right" reasons stand in the way of making progress. Chances are it will rarely *feel* right, but in retrospect will be right.

If you don't have everything you need to make your finances operate efficiently, if you don't have a complete team, or if you haven't figured out how to make it all work, then the time to get started is now. Put another way, if you are having problems managing finances, or if you aren't getting timely financial reports, something is wrong and needs to be fixed.

Finally, please understand that this book is really part of a larger picture. It's not enough to have everything put together, because they're really just a platform. It is now your job to take this information and use it to benefit the ministry under your care, and this means understanding what the numbers mean, looking at options the ministry has for outreach and growth, creating a strategic plan, understanding how things will unfold financially under that plan, and understanding how you'll need to fundraise to support that plan.

My heartfelt desire is that this book will serve as your checklist for finding financial management gaps, prioritizing the needs, and finding the solution. Short of speaking with you one-on-one for more detailed help, these are the things that equip you with the resources you need to steward the ministry the Master as entrusted to you, his servant.

NOTES

NOTES

RESOURCES

**Capterra's Top Church Management
Software Products Listing**

http://www.capterra.com/church-management-software

Looking for the right "what" to put into your financial systems? This is a great place to start.

The Church Network

http://www.thechurchnetwork.com

This organization was formerly known as the National Association of Church Business Administration. True to its former name, it is the professional association for church administrators. What makes it so valuable is the amount of resources it has: books, training, and a page of professional resources for hire are all found on their website.

Church Law and Tax

http://www.churchlawandtax.com

Richard Hammar's website is the go-to place for church law, offering both free and premium resources.

NEXT Church

https://nextchurch.net/church-administration-blog/

NEXT Church is a project of Village Presbyterian Church in Prairie Village, Kansas, and the blog has excellent entries on church administration.

STARTChurch

https://www.startchurch.com

Pastor Raul Rivera has a wonderful ministry in the areas of church taxes and church law, with an occasional foray into finance. What makes his blog valuable is that he has excellent stories that support his topics.

Tower Ministry Finance

http://www.towerministryfinance.com/FreedomToServe

More resources are available at this book's web page.

Ultimate Church Suppliers Guide

http://ultimatechurchsuppliersguide.com

This resource from The Church Network is a repository of resources and services available to churches and ministries.

Acknowledgements

To the family God has given me: Kim and Bruce, David and Joo Young, Sungjin and Joelle, Seungyup and SuJung, Jaein and Jinhwa, Jeff and Cat, and all the nieces and nephews that have brought joy into my life.

To so many faithful friends, thank you from the bottom of my heart.

To my spiritual mentors: Rev. Valerie Bailey Fischer, Rev. Jacob Smith and the pastoral team at Calvary-St. George's, Rev. Sang Il Park, and Rev. Sung Jun Kim; each one has taught me, encouraged me, and nurtured me in faith.

To my assistant, Michelle Richardson, whose service to clients and administrative support gave me the space to write.

To colleagues who contributed to different sections:
Elizabeth Picarella (www.picarellainsurance.com) for her comments on insurance and risk,

Juliana Zhu (www.julianazhu.com) for her contributions to the section on attorneys,

Joel Field (www.fieldfinancialstrategies.com) for his input on retirement planning,

Larry Bennett (www.nycbennetts.com) on taxes, and

Alex Mottorshead (treasurer) and Nathan Rose (finance committee chair) at Calvary-St. George's Church for their perspectives on their roles in church financial leadership and investment management.

A SPECIAL REQUEST

As I complete this book, 25 million North Koreans are suffering from lack of food—physical and spiritual—due to an oppressive regime. The 300,000 Christians there are regularly persecuted and forced to practice their faith in hiding. Yet at the beginning of the last century, Pyongyang, its capital, was known by missionaries as the "Jerusalem of the East" due to its thriving Christian population. One of my personal prayers is for the liberation of the people and reunification of North and South Korea into one nation.

Since 2005, a special organization has made this their mission. **Liberty in North Korea** has been working hard to help North Korean refugees escape and resettle, and to engage international leaders and the media by bringing attention to the plight of North Koreans, all of which will help continue to put pressure on the North Korean government to give freedom to their people.

I've written this book with the hope that it will literally be valuable to you—that in a few hours you will have information and a strategy that will save you a significant amount of time and your ministry a lot of money. If it has been helpful, would you give a gift to Liberty in North Korea so that light and life will one day return to Pyongyang and the people of North Korea? And by the way, you already have given without realizing it! My personal tithe is going to them as my way of supporting their front-line work.

Visit www.TowerMinistryFinance.com/FreedomToServe to learn more about their work and for the donation link.

Thank you so much!

ABOUT THE AUTHOR

Jonathan Ankney is the founder of Tower Ministry Finance, the church and ministry division of Small Business CFO, Inc., an outsourced CFO and accounting services firm based in New York City.

Hailing from the countryside of western Pennsylvania, his original plan was to become a professional musician as a classical trumpet player. After several years of dividing his time between freelance music and administrative temping, he changed course and enrolled in the MBA in Arts Administration program at Binghamton University. He expanded his educational goals there, and in spite of initially grappling to get his musician brain around accounting concepts the first month of business school, added finance as a second major.

After graduate school he worked in financial management and accounting in orchestras and small businesses, until 2004 when he launched Small Business CFO. After nearly 10 years of working with churches and ministries he concluded that his creative upbringing, formal business education, and passion for helping ministries required a new initiative, so in 2017 he added Tower Ministry Finance to offer church plants, churches without full-time professional finance staff, and small ministries access to financial expertise and services they typically could not have.

In his role as chief financial officer, controller, and consultant to these organizations, he combines his creative years with decades of experience in finance to create robust systems and procedures, develop clear financial reports, and train ministry staff and volunteers so that they can perform day-to-day financial tasks accurately and confidently.

Jonathan is an active Toastmaster, avid bicyclist, and enjoys spending time with his family. He resides in New York City and attends Calvary Church in the parish of Calvary-St. George's in the City of New York.

www.ingramcontent.com/pod-product-compliance
Lightning Source LLC
Chambersburg PA
CBHW061736020426
42331CB00006B/1262